101 Aggie Facts
Things Every Longhorn Should Know

KYLE UMLANG

DEDICATION

This book is dedicated to my loving wife for putting up
with my College Football and Texas Longhorn obsession
for more than a decade.

CONTENTS

ACKNOWLEDGMENTS

First off, I would like to thank all of my followers on Twitter for liking, supporting and sharing my stats. I also want to thank Aggies, for without them this book would not exist. Also, thanks to my family for raising a divided household and enabling this whole rivalry thing.

A special thank you goes to all the sports data websites that provide the means for my stats and to Blinkin Riley for not only his contributions to the sports stats world, but also for starting the #AggieFactThursday movement.

I would like to give one last thanks to my Dad and little brother for not only being Aggies, but for watching, living and loving that special rivalry with me every Thanksgiving for as long as I can remember.

1 THE RIVALRY

Fact #1

From the Texas Constitution, 1876: the legislature, as soon as practicable, was to establish, organize, and provide for the maintenance and support of a "university of the first class".

Texas A&M was created in 1871.

Fact #2

In the first seven games of the rivalry, Texas kept the Aggies scoreless while racking up 157 unanswered points.

A&M reached 157 points in the rivalry during the 32nd meeting.

Fact #3

Texas has scored more points against Texas A&M than any other school has in history.

The Longhorns have scored 2,297 points against the Aggies in their 118 matchups averaging 19.5 points a game, while Texas A&M averages 12.3 points a game against the Longhorns.

Fact #4

The most points Texas A&M has ever scored against Texas is 42 points (1985).

The Longhorns have scored 42 points or more against the Aggies 14 different times, with their largest score coming in 1977 when they won 57-28.

Fact #5

By 1952, Texas had already beaten Texas A&M more times than the Aggies would ever beat the Longhorns in the rivalry's history (38).

Fact #6

Texas A&M has given up 921 points to Texas at Kyle Field while only scoring 778 against them.

Their record at home against the Longhorns is 22-25-2 (0.469).

Fact #7

Number of times Texas held
Texas A&M to under 7 points:
40

Number of times Texas A&M
beat Texas ever:
37

Fact #8

Number of times Texas beat
A&M in football during an
even numbered year:
44

Number of times A&M beat
Texas in football during an
even or odd numbered year:
37

Fact #9

Number of times Texas beat
Texas A&M in Football,
Basketball and Baseball in the
same year:
48

Number of times Texas A&M
beat Texas in just Football:
37

Fact #10

For Texas A&M to rack up 3 different decades where they have a better winning percentage than the Longhorns, they would have to go back to the 1930s.

Fact #11

If Texas A&M was spotted a touchdown in every game of the football rivalry with Texas, the Longhorns would still lead the series 60-53-5 (0.530).

Fact #12

If the President pardoned all of Texas A&M's losses from when they were strictly a military school, they would still have a losing record to Texas.

Fact #13

There are only 5 years out of 118 years of the football rivalry that Texas A&M can cherry pick from to give themselves a winning head-to-head record:

1975, 1979, 1983, 1984, 1985

Fact #14

Darrell K. Royal coached the Texas Longhorns from 1957-1976, where he never had a losing season.

During his tenure, Texas won 11 conference championships, made 16 bowl game appearances & had as many National Championships (3) as losses to Texas A&M (3).

Fact #15

Only 2 Texas A&M Head Coaches have a winning record over Texas during their tenure.

12 Texas A&M Head Coaches never saw a single victory over the Longhorns.

Fact #16

If Texas A&M was given the opportunity to rewrite history and start the rivalry from the beginning of any decade of their choosing, they still would not have a winning record against Texas.

2 ALL-TIME

Fact #17

If the coronavirus made every College Football season "conference-only" indefinitely, the only way Texas A&M would be able to catch up to Texas' All-Time win count is if the Longhorns ended their football program.

Even then, they wouldn't catch up until the year 2047.

Fact #18

Not counting pre-integration stats, Texas has...

- 37 more Wins
- 8 more 10-Win Seasons
- 23 more All-Americans
- 19 more weeks Ranked #1
- 8 more Top 5 Finishes
- 7 more Top 10 Finishes
- 5 more Conference Titles
- 5 more Bowl Wins
- 3 more BCS/NY6 Wins
- 2 more National Titles
- 5 more Heisman Winners & Runner Ups

...than Texas A&M.

Fact #19

Texas A&M is 1-8 (0.111)
All-Time when they play in a
game presented by
ESPN's College Gameday.

Only Georgia Tech (0.000) has
a worse record when making at
least five appearances.

Fact #20

There is not a single football player in Texas A&M's entire 125-year program history who has more Total Yards, Total Touchdowns or Bowl Wins in their career than Sam Ehlinger.

Fact #21

Texas A&M's best decade in
the last century was 1990-1999
where they went 94-28-2
(0.766).

58 different team decades have
been better including 4
different Texas decades:

'70-'79
'40-'49
'60-'69
'00-'09

Fact #22

Only 16 Power 5 schools have had a longer football Conference Championship drought than Texas A&M.

Their last Conference Championship was in 1998, when they beat Kansas State 36-33 in the Big 12 Championship.

Fact #23

In All Time Win %, Texas
A&M is closer to:

Bowling Green
Louisiana Tech
Middle Tennessee
San Diego State
South Florida
Southern Mississippi
Old Dominion
Texas St
Toledo
Troy
Western Kentucky

…than they are to Texas.

Fact #24

Who has the better Win % against each FBS Conference

- AAC - Texas
- ACC - Texas
- BIG12 - Texas
- B1G - Texas
- CUSA - Texas
- IND - Texas
- MAC - Texas A&M *
- MWC - Texas
- PAC12 - Texas
- SEC - Texas
- SUN - Texas

* Texas has never played a MAC opponent

Fact #25

Texas A&M has been ranked #1 in the AP Poll 7 times in their history, the last time being 1957.

Texas has been ranked #1 in the AP Poll 45 times, the last time being 2008.

Fact #26

Texas has more All Americans, National Championships, Weeks ranked Top 5, Weeks ranked Top 10, Heisman Winners, Heisman Runner Ups, Heisman Finalists and 10-win seasons in the last 40 years than Texas A&M has in their entire history.

Fact #27

The Blue Bloods of College Football are Texas, Oklahoma, Nebraska, USC, Notre Dame, Ohio State, Michigan and Alabama.

All-Time Record against the Blue Bloods:

Texas 88-71-6 (0.552)
A&M 59-129-5 (0.313)

Fact #28

Only 6 teams have more
unanimous All-Americans than
Texas (25) All-Time and only
3 teams have more in the last
20 years (8).

23 teams have more
unanimous All-Americans than
Texas A&M (9) All-Time.

Fact #29

Texas has finished in the Top 10 in the NCAA Division 1 Directors' Cup 23 times All-Time.

Texas A&M has finished 6 times All-Time.

Fact #30

UTEP has scored more points on Texas A&M than they have scored on Texas, even though they've played the Longhorns twice as many times.

Fact #31

Texas A&M has won 12+ games in a season one time in their history (1992).

Texas has won 12+ games three times since 2005.

Fact #32

Texas A&M has played more FCS teams in the past 5 seasons than Texas has played All-Time.

Fact #33

UCLA has nearly 3 times more Top 5 Finishes than Texas A&M.

Fact #34

At their current win rate, Texas
is due to arrive at the 1,000
win mark sometime during the
2029 season. Texas A&M will
arrive in 2051.

3 THE SEC

Fact #35

Texas A&M lost their last game as a member of the Big 12 Conference to Texas 27-25 on 11/24/2011.

Texas A&M lost their first game as a member of the Southeastern Conference to Florida 20-17 on 9/8/2012.

Fact #36

Louisiana Lafayette is 1-68 (0.014) against teams that are currently in the SEC. That one win is against Texas A&M.

Fact #37

No SEC team has played as
many FCS teams as Texas
A&M has since joining the
SEC in 2012.

Fact #38

The Texas A&M athletics department won 38% less Conference Championships during their first eleven athletic seasons in the SEC (29) than they did in their last eleven athletic seasons in the Big 12 (47).

Fact #39

Texas A&M and Vanderbilt
are the only SEC teams that
have not won an
SEC Championship or
SEC Division Title in Football.

Fact #40

Since joining the SEC, Texas A&M has racked up an impressive 90 wins:

11 vs. FCS
21 vs. G5
27 vs. P5 w/out winning record
8 vs. Arkansas, South Carolina or Vanderbilt with a winning record.

Only 25.6% of A&M's wins were against P5 teams w/ winning records not named Arkansas, South Carolina or Vanderbilt

Fact #41

Teams with more SEC Football Championships than Texas A&M

Alabama
Auburn
Florida
Georgia
Georgia Tech
Kentucky
LSU
Mississippi State
Ole Miss
Tennessee
Tulane

Fact #42

Texas A&M's Conference Record | 1915 – 2022
340-305-25 (0.526)

Southwest Conference
(1915 – 1995)
223-202-25 (0.523)

Big 12 Conference
(1996 – 2011)
69-62-0 (0.527)

Southeastern Conference
(2012 – 2022)
48-41-0 (0.539)

Fact #43

Texas A&M Conference Record at Home | 1915 – 2022
178-131-10 (0.574)

Southwest Conference
(1915 – 1995)
119-85-10 (0.579)

Big 12 Conference
(1996 – 2011)
38-27 (0.585)

Southeastern Conference
(2012 – 2022)
21-19 (0.525)

Fact #44

65% of Texas A&M's conference wins since joining the SEC have come against Arkansas (10), the Mississippi schools (10), South Carolina (8) and Vanderbilt (3).

Fact #45

Texas A&M's Win % against the best two teams in their division:

Last 11 years in B12:
5-17 (0.227)

First 11 years in SEC:
5-17 (0.227)

Fact #46

Since joining the SEC, Texas A&M has more wins over FCS (11) opponents than yearly conference division foes Alabama, Auburn and LSU combined (10).

4 ATHLETICS

Fact #47

Texas vs A&M | All-Time (M & W)

Baseball 245-130-5 (0.651)
Softball 24-22 (0.522)
Volleyball 75-23 (0.765)
Soccer 6-19-2 (0.259)
Basketball 201-110 (0.646)
Football 76-37-5 (0.665)
Tennis 144-29-2 (0.829)
Swimming 126-13 (0.906)

Fact #48

One of the only metrics Texas A&M leads Texas in is Non-FBS wins.

They have played 39 more games against teams that aren't currently one of the 130 Division 1 FBS teams.

Fact #49

Women's Soccer is the only sport in which Texas A&M has a lead against Texas head-to-head.

Fact #50

The coronavirus canceled the remainder of the 2020 Baseball season, where the Aggies and Longhorns were a mere 18 days from squaring off.

If Texas A&M and Texas played EVERY 18 days and the Aggies won 4 out of 5 of those games going forward, they would get on the winning side of the Head-to-Head Record with Texas in the year 2029.

Fact #51

From 1962-2017, Texas A&M
Men's Swimming was winless
head-to-head against Texas.

They broke the streak with a
narrow 3-point victory.

They haven't won since.

Fact #52

Since 1990, Texas has beaten Texas A&M in 8 or more different sports during the same calendar year a record 20 times.

Texas A&M has never beaten Texas in 8 or more sports in the same year.

Fact #53

Using their College World Series win percentage, if Texas A&M appeared in EVERY College World Series from here until the end of time, while Texas was banned forever, the Aggies would reach the Longhorns' number of wins in the year 2170.

Fact #54

Texas Top 5 Finishes in Football during Leap Years:
5

A&M Top 5 Finishes in Football, Basketball & Baseball All-Time:
4

Fact #55

Texas A&M has finished in the Top 5 of a major sport (Football, Basketball & Baseball) 5 times in the last 60 years

2022 – Baseball
2020 – Football
2012 – Football
1993 – Baseball
1989 – Baseball

Texas has done this 40 times in the same time span. No team has done it more.

Fact #56

If after a year of no
ticket/concession revenue due
to coronavirus concerns Texas
had to cancel all sports
indefinitely & Texas A&M
repeated their best season this
millennium in each sport,
here's when they would pass
Texas' winning %

Basketball 2068
Football 2088
Baseball 2181

Fact #57

Texas vs. Texas A&M | All Sports

Last 25 years
Texas leads A&M 234-124-2
(0.653)

Last 15 years
Texas leads A&M 97-53-0
(0.647)

Last 5 years
Texas leads A&M 23-8-0
(0.742)

5 CHAMPIONSHIPS

Fact #58

Texas A&M's last football National Championship is closer to the Emancipation Proclamation than it is to this upcoming season.

Fact #59

Nebraska has twice as many unclaimed football National Championships as Texas A&M has claimed football National Championships.

Fact #60

Austin Peay and Central Arkansas have had more football Conference Championships since 2019 than Texas A&M has had in the last 20 years.

Fact #61

For $6 in 2019, you could have bought a ticket for the Texas A&M Season opener against Texas State.

For $6 the last time Texas A&M won a national title (1940), you could have driven from College Station to Memphis and still had enough money for a hamburger, fries and milk shake at McDonalds, which wouldn't even exist for another 15 years (1955).

Fact #62

Oklahoma A&M changed its name to Oklahoma State in 1957.

To this day, it's still the most successful Agricultural and Mechanical College in NCAA history by earning 23 NCAA Division 1 Championships before their name change.

Texas A&M has 17.
Florida A&M has 1.

Fact #63

Texas A&M Football is little brother to Texas mainly because they have less National Championships and a losing H2H record against them.

Using those metrics, 15 additional schools can technically call them little brother as well.

Fact #64

Claimed Football National Championships:

Texas 4
A&M 3

Claimed Football National Championships if schools claimed every meaningless non-reputable #1 ranking from any selector:

Texas 9
A&M 3

Fact #65

Texas A&M Football has a rich history of bringing in head coaches that perform better at other schools:

3 National Championships have been won at other schools by head coaches before arriving at Texas A&M.

8 have been won at other schools by head coaches after departing Texas A&M.

Fact #66

Since Texas Football won its last National Championship, they have won 14% of their All-Time wins & 8 other schools have won a National Championship.

Since Texas A&M Football won its last National Championship, they have won 68% of their All-Time wins & 40 other schools have won a National Championship.

Fact #67

The University of Texas has won 25 National Championships in NCAA Sports since 2000.

Texas A&M has only won 17 National Championships in NCAA Sports in its entire collegiate history.

Fact #68

Santa Claus has delivered presents to ~131,000,000,000 children (aged 0-14) since Texas A&M's last National Championship in football, which is the equivalent of 1.28MM sell out home games at Kyle Field.

Fact #69

Immediately after joining the SEC in 2012, Texas A&M claimed 2 National Titles and 2 Conference Titles and slapped them on their stadium wall:

National Titles
• 1919 (computer poll that crowned them 50 years later)
• 1927 (computer poll that crowned them 85 years later)

Conference Titles
• 1997 (lost the Big 12 title game to Nebraska 54-15)
• 2010 (not even in Big 12 title game)

Fact #70

Does Texas A&M have more Football Conference Championships than Texas in the last...

decade? – No
2 decades? – No
3 decades? – No
4 decades? – No
5 decades? – No
6 decades? – No
7 decades? – No
8 decades? – No
9 decades? – No

Fact #71

If the entire 51-man roster from the 1939 National Champion Texas A&M Football team each decided to run sprints (5 Field Lengths) every day until the Aggies won their next National Championship, they would have already accumulated enough miles to reach the moon & back.

Fact #72

Years since last played for
Football Conference
Championship:

Texas 5
A&M 25

Years since last played for
Football National
Championship:

Texas 14
A&M 84

6 THIS CENTURY

Fact #73

Since 2000, Texas has started the season 6-0 three times ('05, '08, '09), each time as title contenders with a combined record of 38-2 (0.950), 3 BCS Bowls, 2 National Championship Games & 3 Heisman Finalists.

Texas A&M did it once (2016) & finished the rest of the season 2-5 (0.286).

Fact #74

Texas won more games during the 2018 season (10) than Texas A&M did from either 1946-1949 (8) or 1962-1965 (9).

Fact #75

Since 2000, Texas A&M has had one 10-win season. Only five Power 5 schools have less.

Fact #76

Since 2000, only twice has a Texas A&M quarterback had a completion percentage under 32.5% after completing at least 5 passes.

Both were Kellen Mond.

- 2017 vs Mississippi St
- 2020 vs LSU

Fact #77

Since 2000, Mike Leach has nearly double the wins (9) over Texas A&M than the Aggies have over Alabama, Georgia and LSU combined (5).

Fact #78

Since 2000, Arkansas has had more "Top 15 Finishes" than Texas A&M and has had triple the amount of "10-win Seasons" as the Aggies.

Fact #79

TCU has had more 10-win seasons since 2000 (13) than Texas A&M has had in their entire College Football history (12).

Fact #80

For those Aggies that are optimistic about this upcoming season... In the last 20 years, when ranked in the AP Preseason poll, Texas A&M is 10-26 (0.278) against ranked teams during the regular season.

Fact #81

Texas joined the 900 Win Club in 2018 while Oklahoma joined in 2019.

At their current win rate since joining the SEC, Texas A&M will join the club somewhere in 2034.

If they stopped playing FCS/G5 & only played Power 5 teams, they would join the club in 2047.

Fact #82

When Texas A&M went to the 2019 Texas Bowl, they were the only bowl eligible school at that moment in time with ZERO wins against teams with winning records in Football AND Basketball.

Combined Record of Teams Beaten:

Football 27-57 (0.321)
Basketball 14-25 (.359)

Fact #83

The last time each Top 5 2022
Recruiting Class had both a
Top 5 Class & 10-Win Season
in the same year

Alabama - 2022
Georgia - 2022
Ohio State - 2022
Texas - 2018
Texas A&M - NEVER!

Fact #84

Things that Texas has done in the last 15 seasons that Texas A&M has never done in their 125-year history:

2 Unanimous All-Americans in the same year, 13-win season, Back-to-Back Top 5 recruiting classes, Back-to-Back Top 5 finishes and multiple BCS/NY6 Bowl Wins.

Fact #85

Power 5 programs in Texas with the most wins since 2012

vs. Power 5
67 TCU
63 Texas
59 Baylor
58 Texas A&M
40 Texas Tech

vs. FCS
11 Texas A&M
11 Texas Tech
10 TCU
9 Baylor
0 Texas

Fact #86

Kellen Mond broke nearly every career QB record at Texas A&M in 2020.

To this day, Sam Ehlinger still has 2,000+ more yards of offense and 34 more touchdowns than Kellen.

Fact #87

Since 2000, Texas has finished a season with 4+ losses 12 different times.

In the same time frame, Texas A&M has finished with 4+ losses 21 different times.

Fact #88

Only three Power 5 teams
didn't pad their stats with FCS
opponents since 2010

Notre Dame, Texas & USC

Texas A&M played 11.

7 MISCELLANEOUS

Fact #89

Reveille, the collie mascot for Texas A&M, is commissioned as a five-star general and is the highest-ranking member of the Texas A&M Corps of Cadets.

Fact #90

Texas State has never beaten a Power 5 opponent.

They have 0 Heisman Winners, 0 Heisman Finalists, 0 Heisman Runner Ups, 0 Division 1 Titles, 0 Bowl Game appearances and 0 consensus All-Americans, but they still have the same amount of weeks ranked #1 in the last 60 years as Texas A&M.

Fact #91

Since 1812, there have been more U.S. Capitol breaches than Texas A&M Football National Championships.

Fact #92

During Mack Brown's tenure at Texas, he accounted for 13% of Texas A&M's total losses.

Fact #93

Approximately 323.4 million Americans alive today (97.3% of the U.S. Population) have never seen Texas A&M win a National Championship in football.

Fact #94

Rice has a more recent football Conference Championship than Texas A&M.

Fact #95

Texas A&M's 2020 College Football Playoff resume had more wins against teams that fired their Head Coach than wins against teams with winning records.

Fact #96

In the last 40 years, only 23 NFL first round draft picks have failed to start a game in their professional careers. Texas A&M is responsible for one of them:

1984's 1st round, 25th overall pick Billy Cannon

Fact #97

The Wall Street Journal ranked the most valuable College Football programs and they assessed Texas' brand worth at more than double that of Texas A&M's brand worth.

$1.10B Texas
$541M Texas A&M

Fact #98

If there was a giant malware attack across the United Sates and it erased the first 120 years of Clemson's football records permanently from all College Football databases and record keeping systems, the Tigers would still have a better resume than Texas A&M.

Fact #99

Texas A&M finished in the Top 4 in Football in 2020 and in Baseball in 2022.

If the Aggies continued at their current pace of Top 4 finishes in the 3 major sports (baseball, basketball, football), they will surpass Texas' current Top 4 finish count in the year 3312.

Fact #100

UTEP Football has a winning record over only 1 Power 5 team in their history.

They have 0 wins over Blue Blood programs, 0 Heisman Winners, 0 Heisman Finalists, 0 Division 1 Titles & 0 weeks ranked #1, but they still have a more recent Conference Championship than A&M.

Fact #101

Since Donald Trump was elected president, he has been impeached more times than Texas A&M has beaten Alabama.

101 AGGIE FACTS

ABOUT THE AUTHOR

I'm a proud Texas Longhorn alum who has a passion for College Sports stats and data analysis and visualization. I made a name for myself on Twitter in 2019 with my unique spin on hard-to-find facts and clap backs and then became infamous after the release of my 2021 book 101 Aggie Facts. Like a lot of born and raised Texans out there, I come from a divided Texas/Texas A&M household and family. Aggie jokes have been a part of my entire life and I'm glad I finally have found another medium in which to share mine with the world.

Regarding College Athletics, misconceptions run rampant on social media and my number one goal is to shed light on the topics that are the most incorrectly portrayed and perceived by fans. One of the biggest out there involves the Texas A&M athletic department and the many Aggies who promote a false narrative of their SEC prowess which can only be obtained through years of winning and not just by the patch on their uniforms.

Come find me on Twitter and see for yourself. My true personality shines through in my quick-witted jabs and unique take on stats. I always promote the hard work of others in the sports stats field and try to follow those who show the same interests and passions I hold. I hope you not only learn something new about Aggies in this book, but that you share what you've learned with an Aggie you know.

Lastly, just so we're clear, Texas A&M has never and will never run the state of Texas.

Made in the USA
Columbia, SC
15 December 2023

28638452R00065